ROOTBOUND

Break Free from Feeling Stuck
It's your time to THRIVE

MB Gustitus

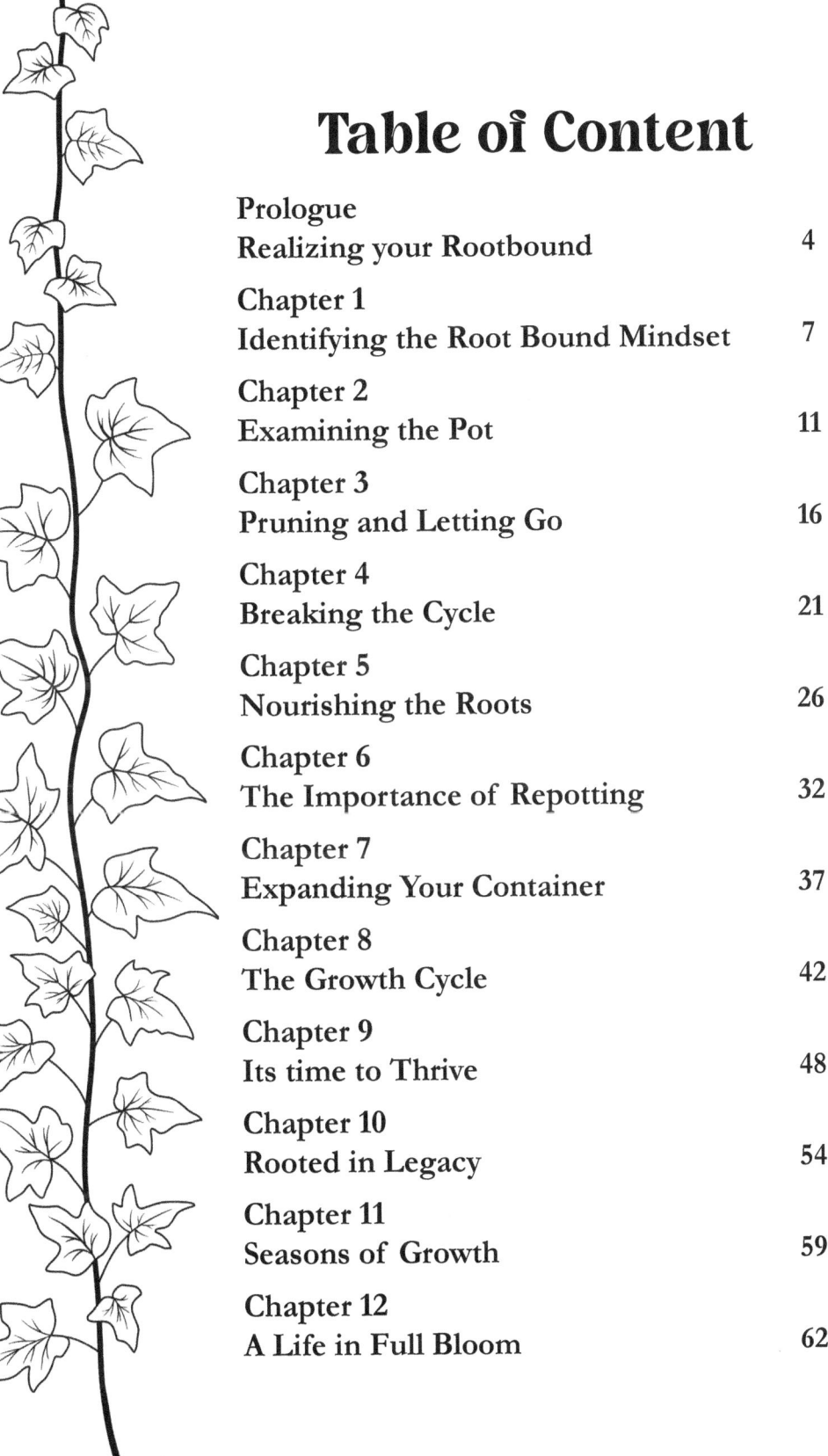

Table of Content

Prologue
Realizing your Rootbound.

Have you ever felt it? That faint tug, like someone gently pulling at the sleeve of your shirt, whispering, "You were made for something more." It's not loud, not at first. It's just a feeling, almost like a nudge in the wrong direction—or so you think. But as time goes on, the tug gets stronger. Louder. Until one day, you can't ignore it anymore.

For me, recognizing I was rootbound wasn't a single moment or a dramatic event. It was more like a slow, growing ache—a sense of being stuck in something that used to fit me perfectly but now felt a little too tight. I was in a career I loved, surrounded by people I cared about deeply, doing work that, by all accounts, should have been fulfilling. But something had shifted. I found myself looking backward, reminiscing about how things "used to be" instead of being excited about what could come next. At the same time, I noticed other relationships beginning to feel strained. When people don't grow together, there's often a reckoning. Sometimes one person wishes the other would catch up, while the other silently hopes they'll just stop growing altogether. The tension was undeniable. I realized that my desire to stretch, to expand, was unsettling to some of the people closest to me. And the truth is, it was unsettling to me too. The push and pull of growth was both exhilarating and isolating, forcing me to confront not only my own fears but also the shifting dynamics in my world.

There's a particular pain that comes with being rootbound. At first, it's subtle, like a little discomfort you can shrug off. But gradually—then suddenly—it starts to consume you. The tangled roots of old beliefs, outdated relationships, and misplaced priorities begin to cut off your potential. You find yourself playing small, convincing yourself that maybe you're just asking for too much. The things that once nurtured you start to feel like they're holding you back, and the impact you know you're capable of making begins to feel out of reach.

I remember standing in the middle of it all—successful, outwardly thriving, and quietly withering. I knew I wasn't making the difference I was meant to make, and the thought of staying where I was filled me with one thing I couldn't ignore: regret. I knew that if I didn't listen to that tug, if I didn't trust the whisper that kept saying, "There's more for you than this," I would look back on my life and wish I had been braver.

This book was born from that moment of clarity, from the pain and frustration of realizing I'd outgrown the pot I was living in. It's not a guide written from a place of perfection—it's a roadmap created from the twists and turns, the messy middles, and the beautiful breakthroughs of learning to trust that voice and give my roots the space they needed to grow.

If you've ever felt like your world has gotten a little too small, like the edges of your pot are closing in and your roots are starting to tangle, this book is for you. It's an invitation to pause, to reflect, and, when the time feels right, to repot yourself in a container that fits the person you are becoming.

Growth isn't easy, and it isn't always pretty. But it's worth it. And the life waiting for you on the other side? It's more than you can imagine.

So grab a cup of coffee, settle in, and let's start untangling those roots. You weren't made to stay stuck— you were made to grow.

Chapter 1
Identifying the Rootbound Mindset

Let me tell you about the day I met my match: a potted plant.

Now, I'm no gardener. My thumbs are as green as a ripe banana—which is to say, not at all. But there it was, this poor plant sitting in the corner of my yard, its leaves drooping, and its pot cracked on one side. I had rescued it from some overambitious spring cleaning weeks ago, promising myself I'd figure out how to save it. And, true to form, I promptly forgot about it. Until that day.

Out of curiosity (or guilt), I tipped the pot over and tried to pull the plant out. What I saw made me gasp. The roots were tangled so tightly that they looked like a knotted ball of yarn, strangling themselves. There was no room left for them to grow. That plant wasn't dying because it was neglected—though I'm sure that didn't help. It was stuck, trapped by the very pot that was supposed to help it thrive.

Does that sound familiar? Maybe not the plant part, but the feeling? That sense of being stuck, constricted, unable to stretch into your full potential because the container you're in is too small? Yeah, me too.

The Pot We Outgrow

We all start with a pot that fits us just fine. Maybe it's a job that challenges us, a relationship that fulfills us, or a mindset that serves us well. But as we grow, those containers don't always grow with us. And before we know it, we're rootbound...restricted by our own comfort zones, habits, or fears. The very things that once nurtured us start to hold us back.

For me, that pot looked like a long, successful career in leadership. I'd built a team, achieved milestones, and earned accolades. But somewhere along the way, I realized I wasn't growing anymore. I was maintaining. I was comfortable, sure, but I was also stuck. My roots were bumping up against the edges of my pot, and it was time to break free.

Recognizing the Signs

So how do you know if you're rootbound? Here are a few signs:

- **Stagnation:** You're not learning or growing. Every day feels like a rerun of the same show.

- **Frustration:** You feel restless or dissatisfied, like something's missing.
- **Exhaustion:** Even the things you used to love feel draining because they've lost their spark.
- **Fear of Change:** You catch yourself clinging to the familiar, even when you know it's not working anymore.

If you're nodding along right now, take heart. Being rootbound isn't a failure; it's a natural part of growth. The challenge is recognizing it and having the courage to do something about it.

The Power of Self-Awareness

The first step in breaking free is self-awareness. You've got to get honest with yourself about where you are and where you want to go. For me, that meant asking tough questions: Am I truly happy, or just comfortable? Am I growing, or just surviving? What would it look like to repot myself?

These questions aren't easy - they will push you to confront truths you might rather ignore. But they'll also illuminate the path forward. Because here's the thing: growth starts with discomfort. And discomfort is just another word for opportunity.

The Potential for Growth

Imagine what would happen if you gave your roots the space to expand. If you planted yourself in a bigger pot, with richer soil and more sunlight. What could you achieve? Who could you become?

The journey to thriving isn't about abandoning who you are; it's about becoming more of who you are meant to be. It's about recognizing that you deserve more—more space, more growth, more life.

I'm sharing this because I've been there. I've felt the ache of outgrowing my pot and the fear of leaving it behind. But I've also experienced the freedom and joy that come with planting myself in a new space. And I want that for you, too.

This chapter is just the beginning. Together, we're going to explore how to break free from the constraints that hold you back and create a life where you can truly flourish. So grab a shovel—metaphorically speaking—and let's get to work. It's time to repot your life and let your roots stretch.

Because the truth is…you were made to grow. And your best life? It's just one bigger pot away.

Chapter 2
Examining the Pot

Have you ever stopped to think about the "pot" you're living in? I don't mean your actual home or office—I'm talking about the framework of your life. The job you're in, the habits you've formed, the relationships you're a part of. That pot. For a while, it works. It's just the right size, providing structure, security, and enough room to grow. But what happens when you outgrow it? Spoiler alert: it's not pretty.

I know because I've been there. I stared at my metaphorical pot, realizing it was no longer big enough to hold my dreams, my energy, or even my enthusiasm for Monday mornings (among many other things). But instead of doing something about it right away, I did what most of us do—I ignored it. I told myself things like, "This is fine. I should be grateful. Other people would kill for this pot." Sound familiar?

When the Pot Holds You Back

Here's the tricky thing about our pots: they're sneaky. At first, they're wonderful—they give us stability and a place to root ourselves. But over time, they become our limits. We stop noticing how cramped they've become because we're so used to the shape of them. It's like living in a too-small pair of shoes—you convince yourself it's normal to feel a little pinched.

For me, the pot that held me back was fear. Fear of failing if I left my comfort zone. Fear of what people would think if I dared to want more. Fear of making a change and regretting it. And let me tell you, fear makes for a terrible gardener. It stunts your growth and whispers, "Stay where you are; it's safer here."

Signs Your Pot Needs an Upgrade

So how do you know if your pot is holding you back? Here are a few telltale signs:

- **You're Playing Small:** You avoid taking risks because the stakes feel too high.
- **You're Uninspired:** The things that used to excite you now feel like a chore.
- **You're Resentful:** Instead of appreciating your current circumstances, you feel trapped by them.

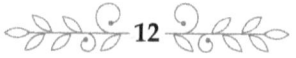

- **You've Lost Sight of Your Why:** The passion or purpose that once guided you is buried under a pile of "shoulds."

If any of this resonates, don't beat yourself up. The fact that you're noticing these feelings is a good thing. It means your roots are calling for more space to grow.

My Turning Point

I remember the moment I realized my pot wasn't working anymore. It wasn't just one thing; it was a thousand little things that added up to a feeling of imbalance. I was overstretched, overstressed, and overwhelmed. The work I had once loved now felt like an endless cycle of putting out fires, and the impact I'd been so proud to make felt like it was slipping through my fingers.

At the same time, I felt this pull—a longing, even—to build on everything I'd already done. I didn't want to abandon the work; I wanted to align it with the person I had become. It was like my roots were calling for a deeper connection to my purpose, a pot that matched the growth I'd experienced internally. But to do that, I had to let go of the pot I'd outgrown. And that's no small thing.

Choosing a Better Pot

Here's the thing about upgrading your pot: it's not just about finding something bigger. It's about finding something better. Something that aligns with who you are and who you're becoming. That might mean a new job, a fresh perspective, or even a complete overhaul of your priorities. The key is to choose a container that allows you to grow, not one that keeps you stuck.

And yes, it's scary. Leaving the pot you know for the unknown is like repotting a plant—it's messy, uncomfortable, and you might lose a few leaves in the process. But the alternative is staying rootbound, and you and I both know that's not where you're meant to be.

Action Steps to Examine Your Pot

Let's get practical. Here are a few steps to help you examine your current pot and decide if it's time for an upgrade:

1. **Take Inventory:** Write down the areas of your life—work, relationships, personal growth, health. Are you thriving, or just surviving?
2. **Ask Hard Questions:** What's holding you back? Is it fear, comfort, or something else? Be honest with yourself.
3. **Imagine the Alternative:** If you could

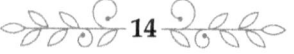

design your ideal pot, what would it look like? What would it give you that your current one doesn't?

4. **Start Small:** You don't have to leap out of your pot all at once. Start by loosening the soil—have a conversation, explore a new opportunity, or try something outside your comfort zone.

Repotting isn't easy, but it's worth it. Because when you give yourself the room to grow, amazing things happen. You rediscover passions you thought you'd lost. You build confidence by stepping into the unknown. And you create a life that feels expansive and full of possibility.

So here's my challenge to you: Take a hard look at your pot. Is it nurturing you, or is it holding you back? If it's the latter, it's time to get your hands dirty and start planting yourself somewhere new. Because you deserve more than just surviving—you deserve to flourish.

Chapter 3
Pruning and Letting Go

Let's talk about pruning. And no, I'm not just talking about your overgrown rose bush or the stray hairs in your eyebrows (although, those could probably use some attention too). I'm talking about the art of releasing what no longer serves you—those habits, thoughts, and even relationships that keep you tangled and stuck. Pruning isn't about loss; it's about making room for growth.

Why Pruning is Necessary

Imagine a tree with too many branches. It's trying to send energy everywhere—feeding the weak, the dead, and the dying along with the strong. It's exhausting itself in the process. That tree isn't thriving; it's surviving. When you prune a tree, you're giving it a chance to direct its energy where it matters most. The same goes for us.

For years, I was like that overgrown tree. I held on to everything—tasks, commitments, even friendships that had long stopped being reciprocal. Why? Because letting go felt too hard. I told myself, "What if I need this later? What if letting go makes me seem selfish?" But all I was doing was exhausting myself. My energy was scattered, and I wasn't giving my best to anything or anyone, least of all myself.

Identifying What No Longer Serves You

Here's where it gets tricky: not everything that needs pruning is obvious. Some things, like a toxic relationship or a draining job, stand out like a broken branch. Others, like an outdated belief or a habit that no longer aligns with your goals, are more subtle.

So how do you identify what needs to go? Start with these questions:

- *Does this energize or drain me?* If it leaves you feeling depleted, it's worth reevaluating.

- *Is this aligned with who I am becoming?* Growth means outgrowing some things, and that's okay.

- *Am I holding on out of guilt or fear?* If the answer is yes, it's time to dig deeper.

For me, one of the hardest things to prune was my tendency to say yes to everything. I thought being a full fledged "people pleaser" made me reliable, likable, and indispensable. But all it did was leave me burnt out and resentful. Learning to say no wasn't easy, but it was liberating. Every no became a yes to something that mattered more.

Letting Go to Grow

Letting go isn't just about removing; it's about creating. When you let go of what no longer serves you, you make space for new opportunities, relationships, and possibilities. It's like cleaning out your closet—getting rid of those "maybe someday" outfits to make room for clothes that actually fit and make you feel good.

I once worked with a client who couldn't let go of a business idea that wasn't working. She had poured time, money, and heart into it, but it had become a source of stress rather than fulfillment. We worked together to reframe her mindset, focusing not on what she was losing, but on what she could gain by redirecting her energy. When she finally let it go, she launched a new venture that aligned perfectly with her skills and passions. The difference was night and day.

Techniques for Pruning Your Life

Ready to start pruning? Here are a few techniques to guide you:

1. **The Energy Audit:** Make a list of everything that demands your time and attention. Then, categorize each item as energizing or draining. Focus on keeping the energizers and finding ways to release the drainers.

2. **The 3-Month Rule:** If you haven't used, worn, or truly needed something in the last six months, consider letting it go. This applies to physical clutter and emotional baggage.

3. **The Mirror Test:** Ask yourself, "If someone else were in this situation, what would I advise them to do?" Sometimes, it's easier to see clearly when we step outside our own perspective.

4. **The Gratitude Shift:** Instead of focusing on what you're losing, focus on what you're gaining. Letting go creates space for what's next.

5. **A Release Ritual:** Write down what you're letting go of—whether it's a fear, a relationship, or a limiting belief—and then symbolically release it. Burn it (safely), shred it, or toss it into the ocean. Rituals can make the process feel more tangible.

My Personal Pruning Moment

I'll never forget the time I decided to step away from a long-term commitment that had become a source of stress. It wasn't bad, exactly—it just wasn't good anymore. But walking away felt like betraying a part of myself. When I finally did it, I felt a mix of relief and fear. The relief was immediate; the fear faded over time. And in its place? Freedom. The kind of freedom that comes when you realize you're not just surviving—you're thriving.

Why Pruning Matters

Pruning isn't just about cutting away the dead weight; it's about nurturing what remains. It's about giving yourself permission to focus on what truly matters, to align your energy with your values, and to grow into the fullest version of yourself.

When you prune your life, you're not just letting go—you're stepping into a new season of growth. You're saying, "I deserve to thrive." And thriving isn't just about adding more to your life; it's about making space for what really counts.

So grab your metaphorical pruning shears and take a good look at your life. What's taking up space that could be better used for growth? What's keeping you stuck? And most importantly, what's waiting to bloom once you let it go? Because the best version of you is waiting—and it's time to make room for it.

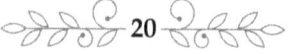

Chapter 4
Breaking the Cycle

Let's get real for a minute—breaking out of old patterns isn't just hard; it's downright terrifying. It's like being asked to karaoke in front of a packed bar when you've never sung outside your shower. You know you're tone-deaf, the mic feels like a hot potato in your hands, and the only thing scarier than starting is stopping in the middle. But once the music starts and you just go for it? Magic happens. The longer you hesitate, the harder it feels. Most of the time, staying stuck is scarier than stepping into the unknown.

The Weight of Limiting Beliefs

We all carry limiting beliefs. They're like invisible weights, holding us back from taking that leap. Maybe it's the voice in your head that says, "You're not good enough." Or the fear that whispers, "What if you fail?" These beliefs might have started as self-protection, but over time, they've become the destructive weeds that choke us out and keep us down.

I'll never forget the moment I realized how much power I had given to my limiting beliefs. I was facing a big opportunity—one that scared me and excited me in equal measure. But instead of saying yes, I found myself listing all the reasons why I wasn't ready. I convinced myself that I needed more experience, more time, more validation. It wasn't until I stopped to reflect that I realized: the only thing holding me back was me.

Tools to Break Free

So how do we break free from these invisible chains? Here are a few ways to start breaking the cycle of limiting beliefs:

1. **Reflective Journaling:** There's something powerful about putting pen to paper. Start by writing down the beliefs that feel like they're holding you back. Then, challenge them. Ask yourself, "Is this really true? Where did this belief come from?" Often, you'll find that these stories aren't rooted in reality but in fear.

2. **Join Communities of Like-Minded People:** Surround yourself with others who are focused on growth and positivity. Their energy and encouragement can help you see what's possible.

3. **Try New Things:** Whether it's a new hobby, a class, or just a small change in your routine, stepping out of your comfort zone can build confidence and open doors.

4. **Read Empowering Books or Listen to Podcasts:** Immerse yourself in content that challenges your perspective and inspires action. Knowledge can be a powerful antidote to fear.

5. **Hire a Professional Coach or Therapist:** Sometimes, we need a guide to help us navigate the tough stuff. A coach or therapist can provide tools and support to overcome limiting beliefs and decisions.

Courage as the Gateway to Growth

Breaking the cycle starts with courage. And let's be honest: courage isn't the absence of fear; it's the decision to move forward despite it. Every time you step into discomfort, you're proving to yourself that you can handle it. And every time you handle it, your confidence grows.

Let me tell you about the time I accepted the challenge of doing a live stand-up comedy routine outside of Boston. If you've never done stand-up, let me paint you a picture: there's no safety net. It's just you, the microphone, and an audience that will either laugh with you or stare blankly as your soul leaves your body. The fear

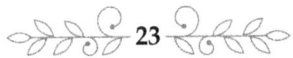

of failure feels like death. I was absolutely terrified. My heart was racing, my palms were sweaty, and I questioned my sanity more than once. But I did it.

Not only did I do it—I crushed it. The laughter from the audience was like fuel to my soul. I walked off that stage feeling invincible. What I didn't realize at the time was that this single act of courage would become the catalyst for so many other brave decisions in my life. When you raise the lid on your courage, you'll find that you are willing be brave more easily and more often. That night taught me that fear might always be there, but it doesn't have to stop you.

Action Steps to Break the Cycle

Ready to start breaking free? Here's how to begin:

1. **Identify Your Patterns:** Take a close look at the beliefs or habits that feel like they're keeping you stuck. Write them down.
2. **Challenge Your Fears:** Ask yourself, "What's the worst that could happen? And if it does, can I handle it?" Spoiler alert: you probably can.
3. **Take One Small Step:** You don't have to overhaul your life overnight. Start with one action that moves you closer to freedom.

4. **Join Forces:** Seek out a community, coach, or friend who can support and encourage you along the way.

5. **Celebrate Your Wins:** Every step forward is worth celebrating, no matter how small. Progress is progress.

Breaking the cycle of limiting beliefs isn't just about overcoming fear—it's about reclaiming your power. It's about stepping into a life where you're not just surviving but thriving. And, most importantly, it's about proving to yourself, over and over, that you are capable of so much more than you think.

So here's my challenge to you: What's one belief or fear you're ready to let go of? Write it down. Challenge it. And then take that first step toward breaking free. Because the truth is: you weren't made to stay stuck. You were made to grow.

Chapter 5
Nourishing the Roots

Let's talk about roots. Not the kind you cover with dirt in your garden, or (in my case) in your hairdressers chair, but the kind that anchor your life. Your roots are the foundation of everything you do—your energy, your relationships, your work, and your sense of purpose. And like any plant, if your roots aren't nourished, everything above ground starts to wither.

The tricky thing about roots: they're often invisible. You don't see them when you're running from meeting to meeting or juggling a million responsibilities. But they're there, quietly doing the heavy lifting. When you ignore them, though, they start to weaken. And when they weaken, everything else starts to feel unstable. Often, by the time we realize we have a root problem, all hell has broken loose in one or more areas of our life.

For me, those roots also include my beliefs and values. They are my internal compass, guiding my decisions and helping me stay grounded in who I am, even when life feels chaotic. When I neglect them—when I compromise my values or lose sight of what truly matters to me—everything else starts to feel out of alignment.

The Importance of Self-Care

Self-care is not selfish. Let me say that again for the people in the back: self-care is not selfish. It's survival. It's the water and sunlight your roots need to stay strong. But self-care isn't always bubble baths and spa days (though those are great). Sometimes, it's as simple as getting enough sleep, saying no to things that drain you, or eating something that didn't come out of a vending machine.

For me, self-care wasn't just uncomfortable—it felt downright unnatural. I was so used to being a giver, not a taker. My default mode was trying to be everything to everyone, people-pleasing out of fear of rejection or being disliked. But eventually, I reached a point where my roots required more than I could give. I had been pouring so much into everyone else's pot that my own was running dry.

Self-care meant setting boundaries and, even harder, having the courage to enforce them. It also meant releasing the need to please others at the expense of myself. These weren't easy lessons to learn, but they were necessary. Over time, I started to see self-care not as an indulgence, but as an essential part of showing up for others in a meaningful way.

Building a Supportive Community

No one grows alone. Even the most resilient plants need good soil, and for us, that soil is our community. The people you surround yourself with have a profound impact on your growth. As Jim Rohn famously said, "You are the average of the five people you spend the most time with." Choose wisely.

During one of the most transformative periods of my life, I joined organizations filled with growth-minded, like-minded individuals. These groups didn't just provide support—they expanded my view of what was possible. Being around people who were committed to their own growth inspired me to dream bigger and take bolder steps. Their encouragement and shared wisdom became an invaluable part of my journey.

I'll never forget a conversation I had with a friend during one of my low points. She looked me in the eye and said, "You don't have to do this alone." It was such a simple statement, but it hit me like a ton of bricks. I had been so focused on proving I could handle everything that I forgot to lean on the people who cared about me.

The Power of Small, Consistent Changes

You don't have to overhaul your entire life to nourish your roots. Growth happens in small, consistent steps. It's about choosing one thing—just one—that you can do today to take care of yourself or strengthen your foundation.

For example, I started a daily gratitude practice. Every night, I wrote down three things I was grateful for. At first, it felt a little silly, like I was just going through the motions. But over time, it shifted my perspective. I started to notice the small joys in my day—a kind word from a friend, a beautiful sunset, or even just a good cup of coffee. That gratitude practice became a cornerstone of my self-care routine, reminding me to focus on what's good and abundant in my life.

Action Steps to Nourish Your Roots

If you're ready to strengthen your foundation, here's where to start:

1. **Check In With Yourself:** Take a moment to ask, "What do I need right now?" Listen to the answer, even if it surprises you.
2. **Prioritize Rest:** Whether it's sleep, downtime, or just a break from your to-do list, give yourself permission to recharge.

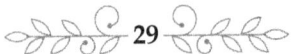

3. **Invest in Your Relationships:** Reach out to the people who matter most to you. Share your time, your attention, and your gratitude.

4. **Join a Growth-Oriented Community:** Surround yourself with people who inspire you and challenge you to grow.

5. **Start Small:** Choose one habit that feels doable and commit to it. Remember, consistency beats perfection.

6. **Celebrate Your Progress:** Every step you take to nourish your roots is worth celebrating. Growth is a journey, not a destination.

When your roots are strong, everything else flourishes. They don't just help you stand tall—they remind you of what you stand for. Your roots ground you in your values and give you the strength to stay true to yourself, even when life throws challenges your way.

Think about it: when you nourish your roots, you're not just taking care of today—you're setting the stage for a lifetime of growth and resilience. You're creating a foundation that can weather storms, support your dreams, and inspire those around you.

Take a moment to reflect: What are your roots asking for right now? Is it rest, connection, or maybe just a little grace? Start with one small change. Maybe it's a quiet morning with a cup of coffee, a phone call to a friend, or five minutes spent writing down what you're grateful for. Whatever it is, start small, but start today.

Because the impact of nourishing your roots isn't just personal—it's ripple effect reaches everyone you touch. When you thrive, you inspire others to do the same. So go ahead, take that first step. Your roots—and your future self—will thank you.

Chapter 6
The Importance of Repotting

Let's get one thing straight: repotting is messy. It's dirt under your nails, roots and debris everywhere, and that moment of panic when you're pretty sure you've just killed it (and your hopes, dreams, and passions). But it's also essential. Because staying in a pot that's too small doesn't just slow your growth—it stunts it entirely.

Knowing When It's Time to Repot

Recognizing when it's time for a new pot can be tricky. Life doesn't come with a flashing neon sign that says, "Hey! Time to change!" Instead, it comes with subtler clues: you feel restless, stuck, or downright drained. For me, it felt like I was living on rinse and repeat—going through the motions without any real sense of purpose. It was like my eyeglasses were covered in a film that dulled everything around me, preventing me from seeing the world in all its bright, vibrant colors.

I also realized I had hit snooze on my dreams. I was good at my job, I was recognized for my contributions, and it had become a huge part of my identity. But deep down, I knew it wasn't serving me anymore. I wasn't excited or inspired—I was just…there. And that's when I knew: it was time to repot.

The Messy Middle

No one warns you about the messy middle—the in-between stage where you've left your old pot but haven't quite settled into the new one. It's like buying a fish at the pet store. They scoop it out of its familiar tank, plop it into one of those little plastic bags, and hand it to you like, "Here you go—good luck!" The fish can survive in that bag for a little while, sure, but it's not exactly thriving. And if you leave it in there too long? Well, let's just say it's not going to end well and you will be looking for a new fish.

When I left my job—a role I had built my identity around—it felt like I was that fish in the bag. I had left the tank I knew, but I hadn't yet found my way into the new one. It was uncomfortable, disorienting, and more than a little scary. But here's the thing: that bag isn't your final destination. It's just a temporary stop on the way to something better. And when you finally get placed into your new tank, the one with all that extra room to swim? That's when you realize it was worth it.

Transition Stories: Lessons in Change

Let me tell you about a plant I repotted once. (Yes, we're sticking with the plant metaphor. Stay with me.) It had been in the same pot for years, its roots so tangled they'd started growing out the drainage holes. When I finally transferred it to a larger pot, it looked pitiful—droopy leaves, a few broken stems, the works. I remember thinking to myself "I should have just left it where it was – this was a mistake". But after a little time, some water, and a lot of sunlight, it flourished.

The same goes for us. When you step into a new pot—whether it's a job, relationship, or mindset—you might feel a little droopy at first. You might even wonder if you made the wrong choice. But with time, care, and a willingness to adapt, you'll start to thrive in ways you never thought possible.

Actionable Advice for Repotting Your Life

If you're feeling rootbound and ready for change, here are some steps to guide you through the process:

1. **Identify the Signs:** Are you feeling stifled, uninspired, or disconnected? These are clues that your current pot isn't serving you anymore.

2. **Envision the Bigger Pot:** What does growth look like for you? Imagine the job, relationship, or mindset that gives you space to expand.

3. **Take the Leap:** Change is scary, but staying stuck is scarier. Trust yourself enough to step into the unknown.

4. **Embrace the Mess:** Growth isn't linear, and the transition will have its ups and downs. Be patient with yourself.

5. **Seek Support:** Surround yourself with people who believe in your potential and can cheer you on through the messy middle.

Repotting isn't just about giving your roots more space. It's about giving yourself permission to grow into the person you're meant to be. It's about recognizing that while the process might be uncomfortable, it's also transformational.

When you move to a bigger pot, you're not just expanding your physical or emotional space—you're expanding your possibilities. You're saying, "I deserve more. I'm capable of more." Repotting is a bold act of self-belief. It's a declaration that your hopes, dreams, and passions are worth investing in.

Growth doesn't happen in comfort zones. It happens when you challenge yourself to step into the unknown, to embrace the messy middle, and to trust that you're building something better. And yes, it's scary. But it's also exhilarating. Because every time you repot, you give yourself a chance to flourish in new, unexpected ways.

So, if you're feeling rootbound, consider this your sign. It's time to repot. Embrace the mess, trust the process, and watch as you grow into the fullest version of yourself. Your best life is waiting—and it's only a bigger pot away.

Chapter 7
Expanding Your Container

Let's talk about containers. Not the kind you use to store leftovers (although, shoutout to Tupperware for keeping us organized). I mean the metaphorical container that holds your life—your ambitions, your dreams, your growth. Just like a plant needs a pot that matches its size, we need a container that can hold the full scope of who we are becoming. And when that container gets too small? It's time to expand.

Creating a Vision for Your Next Stage of Growth

Growth doesn't happen by accident. It starts with a vision—a clear picture of what you want your next stage to look like. But let me be real: creating a vision can feel intimidating. It's like staring at a blank canvas and being told to paint your masterpiece. Where do you even begin?

I'll never forget my first professional development class. The instructor asked us to write down 50 things we wanted to do before we died. Died? I remember

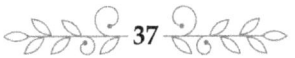

thinking, "I'm here to learn how to write better emails, not contemplate my mortality!" At first, I thought it would be easy—50 things? Piece of cake. But as I stared at the blank page, I realized my container was so small that I struggled to come up with even 10. I started writing things like "learn French"—which, let's be honest, I had no intention of doing then or now. It wasn't just hard—it was eye-opening. My vision for my life was confined, and that exercise pushed me to start dreaming bigger.

Here's the truth: when you allow yourself to imagine what could be, you start to break free from the limits you've placed on yourself. So what if your dreams feel ridiculous or out of reach? Write them down anyway. Want to skydive? Do it. Always dreamed of starting a llama farm? Add it to the list. You're not committing to all of them right now—you're just giving yourself permission to expand.

The Role of Purpose, Values, and Legacy

Expanding your container isn't just about making more space—it's about filling that space with what matters most. That's where purpose, values, and legacy come in. These are the roots of your container, anchoring you in what's meaningful.

- **Purpose:** Why do you do what you do? What gets you out of bed in the morning?
- **Values:** What principles guide your decisions? For me, positive impact is at the top of the list, followed by integrity, authenticity, connection, and growth.
- **Legacy:** How do you want to be remembered? What kind of impact do you want to leave behind?

When I focus on these things, my container naturally expands because I'm building a life that's deeply aligned with who I am. Purpose drives your actions. Values keep you grounded. Legacy reminds you to think beyond yourself. Together, they create a container worth growing into.

Exercises to Clarify Your Vision

If you're ready to expand your container, here are a few exercises to help you clarify your vision:

1. **The Ideal Day Exercise:** Close your eyes and imagine your perfect day from start to finish. Where are you? Who are you with? What are you doing? Write it all down. This exercise helps you identify what truly matters to you.

2. **The Values Audit:** Make a list of your top five values. Then, ask yourself: Are my current choices aligned with these values? If not, what needs to change?

3. **The Legacy Letter:** Write a letter as if it's being read at your 100th birthday celebration. What do you want people to say about the life you've lived and the impact you've had?

4. **The Expansion List:** Write down everything you've been afraid to pursue because it feels too big or too risky. Then, pick one thing and take a small step toward it.

5. **The Vision Board:** Get creative—cut out pictures, draw, or make a digital collage that represents your vision. Seeing it visually can make it feel more real.

My Journey to Expansion

I remember the first time I expanded my container—it was terrifying. I left behind a career that felt safe but stifling to pursue something I was deeply passionate about. At first, I felt like I was floundering, unsure if I could handle the space I'd created for myself. But as I leaned into my purpose and stayed true to my values, I began to thrive. That new container didn't just hold me—it gave me room to grow in ways I never imagined.

Why Expanding Your Container Matters

Expanding your container isn't about perfection or having it all figured out. It's about courage—the courage to dream bigger, to embrace the unknown, and to trust that you're capable of more than you think. When you expand your container, you're saying, "I believe in my potential."

When your container grows, so does your capacity to live a life that aligns with your deepest values and biggest dreams. It's not just about holding space for yourself—it's about holding space for the impact you're here to make. Positive impact doesn't happen by accident; it happens when you create the room to let it flourish.

So, what does your next container look like? Start dreaming, start exploring, and start expanding. Your future self is waiting—and it's time to give them the space they deserve.

Chapter 8
The Growth Cycle

Let's get one thing straight: growth is not a straight line. It's more like a rollercoaster that no one warned you about—full of twists, turns, and occasional upside-down loops that make you question your life choices. But here's the beauty of it: even the messiest parts of the ride contribute to where you're going.

Growth is Not Linear

When I first started my personal growth journey, I had this picture-perfect idea of how it would go: one success after another, building momentum like a well-oiled machine. Spoiler alert: it didn't work that way. Growth looked more like taking two steps forward, one step back, and occasionally tripping over my own feet. It wasn't pretty, but it was progress.

One example stands out. For nearly two years, I worked tirelessly to earn a spot as a coach with a company I had aspired to join for almost a decade. When I finally achieved it, I felt like I was standing on top of the mountain. But within a few months, I realized it wasn't a good fit for me. I felt like a failure. All that time, effort, and energy seemed wasted. I didn't want to admit it—especially to my kids. When I finally told them, in the middle of an ugly cry, their wisdom floored me. "Mommy," they said, "how would you know it wasn't for you if you didn't go this far? Wouldn't you still be wishing you could make it there?" They were right. It wasn't a failure—it was feedback. I thought it was something I wanted to settle down into, but it was just something I needed to pass through on my journey to what was right for me. Has that ever happened to you? You wanted something so badly, and then got it. And then realized it wasn't really what you wanted? It makes me think of a line from one of my favorite Garth Brooks songs, "Sometimes I thank God for...Unanswered Prayers".

Navigating Setbacks with Resilience and Self-Compassion

Setbacks are inevitable. They're not a sign that you're failing; they're a sign that you're in the middle of the process. The key is how you navigate them. Do you let them define you, or do you use them as stepping stones?

One of the hardest lessons I learned was the importance of self-compassion. I used to be my own worst critic. If I stumbled, I'd replay the mistake over and over, beating myself up for not being perfect. But growth doesn't require perfection; it requires persistence. When I started treating myself with the same kindness I'd offer a friend, everything shifted. Mistakes became lessons, and setbacks became opportunities to recalibrate.

This reminds me of a story that originates from ancient Taoist philosophy called "Good Thing, Bad Thing, Who Knows?"

A farmer's horse runs away, and his neighbors say, "How terrible!" He replies, "Good thing, bad thing, who knows?" The horse returns with more horses, and the neighbors exclaim, "How wonderful!" Again, he says, "Good thing, bad thing, who knows?"

Later, while trying to tame one of the new horses, the farmer's son breaks his leg. The neighbors again chime in, "How awful!" and once more, the farmer responds, "Good thing, bad thing, who knows?" A week later, the military comes to the village to recruit all the able-bodied young men for war. The farmer's son is spared because of his injury.

This story isn't just a philosophical exercise; it's a powerful reminder that what feels like a setback in the

moment might actually be paving the way for something better. When we adopt this perspective, we can accept what's happening without getting stuck in negative thinking. It's not about pretending everything is perfect— it's about staying open to the possibility that challenges might hold unexpected opportunities. Growth often works this way—life is lived forward but understood in reverse.

The Importance of Reflection and Recalibration

Growth without reflection is like running a race without a finish line—you're moving, but you're not sure where you're going, and certainly don't know when you have arrived. Reflection allows you to pause, take stock, and adjust your course. It's not about dwelling on the past; it's about learning from it.

One of my favorite tools for reflection is journaling. At the end of each week, I ask myself three simple questions:

1. What went well?
2. What didn't go as planned?
3. What can I do differently next time?

These questions aren't just about identifying wins and losses—they're about understanding patterns, celebrating progress, and making intentional choices moving forward.

 45

My Personal Growth Cycle

Growth required me to stop worrying about what other people thought of me, my choices, and my actions. It required real vulnerability, including the possibility of no longer fitting into circles that were once my comfort zones—even with people closest to me. When you decide to grow, you change the terms of some relationships, and not everyone will be thrilled about it.

Imagine this: You're a plant thriving in a small pot, and suddenly, you outgrow it. Your roots need more space, but your old pot doesn't agree. It's like the pot saying, "Hey, why are you leaving? I thought we had a good thing going!" That's how some relationships feel when you start to grow. You must decide if you're willing to expand anyway. For me, that meant letting go of the fear of rejection and stepping boldly into who I was becoming.

Exercises for Embracing the Growth Cycle

If you're navigating your own growth cycle, here are a few exercises to keep you grounded:

1. **The Setback Reframe:** Write down a recent setback and list three things it taught you. How can you use those lessons to move forward?

2. **The Progress Jar:** Each time you make progress—big or small—write it on a piece of paper and put it in a jar. On tough days,

pull out a few notes to remind yourself of how far you've come.

3. **The Self-Compassion Letter:** Write a letter to yourself as if you were writing to a friend. Acknowledge your challenges, celebrate your efforts, and offer yourself encouragement.

4. **The Pause and Pivot:** Schedule regular check-ins with yourself. Ask: Am I still aligned with my goals? What needs to shift?

Why the Growth Cycle Matters

The growth cycle isn't just about getting from point A to point B; it's about becoming the person you're meant to be along the way. As Søren Kierkegaard said, "Life can only be understood backwards, but it must be lived forwards." The setbacks, recalibrations, and moments of triumph all play a role in shaping your journey.

When you embrace the cycle, you stop fearing the twists and turns. You understand that growth isn't about reaching a destination—it's about evolving, learning, and finding joy in the process. You give yourself permission to stumble, to rise, and to keep moving forward, knowing that every part of the journey has value.

So, where are you in your growth cycle? Wherever you are, know that it's exactly where you're meant to be. Embrace it, learn from it, and trust that you're grow

Chapter 9
Its time to Thrive

Let's talk about thriving. It's a word that sounds like it belongs in a gardening catalog, but in reality, it's what happens when you've done the hard work of breaking through your limitations, expanding your container, and nurturing your roots – its growth in full bloom.

What Does It Mean to Truly Thrive?

To thrive is like being a plant in the perfect pot, under ideal sunlight, with just the right amount of water—not too much, not too little. It's like hitting your Goldilocks zone, where everything aligns just enough for you to grow wildly and unapologetically.

Or, for a more human analogy Thriving is like being the first kid picked for the dodgeball team in 4th grade. You're standing there, pretending to be humble, but inside you're thinking, "I'm unstoppable!" It's not just about being chosen—it's about knowing you've got what it takes to own the game.

Thriving means living in alignment with your purpose, values, and unique gifts. It's about embracing the fullness of who you are and letting that energy ripple out into the world. Thriving doesn't mean you're free from challenges; it means you've built the resilience and mindset to navigate them with grace and intention.

I remember a moment when I truly felt like I was thriving. I had just finished facilitating a retreat for a group of leaders who walked in feeling stuck and left feeling inspired and energized. Watching them reconnect with their purpose and seeing the impact of the tools I shared reminded me why I do what I do. It was overwhelming joy and fulfillment—the kind that bubbles up when you know in your heart you're doing what you were born to do. It was like my divine purpose was being reflected back to me in their transformation. Leaders who doubted themselves walked away with clarity and confidence. Teams that felt disconnected found their rhythm again. Flourishing is watching that spark ignite in others and knowing you played a part in it.

Sustaining Growth

Thriving isn't a destination; it's a state of being that requires ongoing attention. Think of it like tending to a flourishing garden. Even when everything is blooming, you still need to water, weed, and fertilize. The same applies to your personal growth. Reflection, recalibration, consistency, and grit keep the momentum going.

Consistency is the quiet hero of growth. It's not glamorous, but it's what keeps the wheels turning. Showing up day after day, even when it's hard, builds the foundation for sustained growth. Grit, on the other hand, is what gets you through the tough times—the setbacks, the doubts, and the days when you're not sure you can keep going. Together, they create a powerful combination that keeps you moving forward.

Another critical piece is accountability. Having someone to cheer you on, challenge you, and hold you to your commitments makes all the difference. Whether it's a coach, a mentor, or a trusted friend, accountability keeps you grounded and focused.

The Ripple Effects of Personal Growth

Here's the thing about flourishing: it doesn't just impact you. When you grow, everyone around you feels it—your family, your team, your community. Growth has a ripple effect that extends far beyond your own life.

One of the most profound examples of this in my life is the relationship between me and my daughter Brenna. When I really focused on my personal growth and became more self-aware, I realized that my approach to being her mom was flawed. I wanted to describe my "mom style" as intense yet positive—take ownership, no excuses, suck-it-up buttercup, you can handle it! But if you had asked her, she might have described it as controlling, judgmental, and critical. That realization shocked me and moved me to tears…there was a big gap between my good intentions and her reality.

As I grew, I changed. My journey of personal growth shifted me from the inside, and our relationship changed for the better. I remember after one particularly difficult event that included making baklava for Easter, she said, "Thanks, Mom. You're really different. I felt like you supported me and didn't judge me, and I appreciated it." That was a turning point. I don't know if any words spoken to me have ever meant quite so much. Growth isn't just personal; it's deeply relational. And, in case you are wondering – she made an OUTSTANDING Baklava in the end.

Stories of Transformation

One of my favorite examples of thriving comes from a client who came to me feeling completely stuck. They were burned out, disconnected, and unsure of their next steps. Through coaching, we worked on clarifying their values, setting boundaries, and reconnecting with their passions. A year later, they had launched a new business that aligned with their purpose and were making an impact they never thought possible. Watching them step into their potential was a powerful reminder of what's possible when we commit to growth.

Another story comes from my own journey. When I left a safe but stifling job to build something of my own, I wasn't sure how things would turn out. But as I leaned into my values of positive impact and authenticity, everything started to align. The relationships I built, the work I did, and the life I created felt like a true reflection of who I am. That's what thriving feels like—it's not about avoiding risk; it's about embracing the opportunity to grow.

How to Cultivate Flourishing

If you're ready to thrive, here are some steps to help you get there:

1. **Revisit Your Purpose:** Take time to reflect on your why. What drives you? What impact do you want to make?
2. **Celebrate Your Wins:** Acknowledge how far you've come. thriving is about appreciating the journey as much as the destination.
3. **Invest in Relationships:** Surround yourself with people who support, challenge, and inspire you. Growth is a team sport.
4. **Stay Curious:** Keep learning, exploring, and trying new things. Curiosity is a key ingredient in thriving.

5. **Give Back:** When you thrive, share your growth with others. Teach, mentor, or contribute to your community.

Thriving isn't just about living your best life; it's about creating a legacy. It's about showing up fully in the world and using your unique gifts to make a positive impact. When you thrive, you inspire others to do the same. You become a living example of what's possible when we commit to growth.

So, what does thriving look like for you? Maybe it's building a life that feels deeply aligned with your purpose. Maybe it's creating a ripple effect of positivity in your family, team, or community. Whatever it is, know that thriving is within your reach. You've done the hard work of growing your roots and expanding your container—now it's time to bloom.

Chapter 10
Rooted in Legacy

Let's talk about legacy. Not the kind you carve into a building or write on a plaque, but the kind you leave in the hearts and minds of the people you touch. Legacy isn't something you decide to create one day—it's the accumulation of the life you live every day. It's the mark you leave on the world through your actions, your values, and the way you show up.

Tying Growth to Legacy

The fascinating thing about legacy is it's rooted in growth. Every time you choose to grow, you're not just changing yourself, you're planting seeds that will grow long after you're gone. Legacy is about using your growth to create something meaningful for others. It's about asking yourself, What am I building, and who am I building it for?

I think about this a lot when it comes to my own life. Every decision, every moment of courage, every act of kindness contributes to the legacy I'm leaving behind.

But let's be honest: thinking about your legacy can feel overwhelming. So let's break it down. Legacy doesn't have to be grandiose. It can be as simple as the way you make people feel, the lessons you pass on, or the values you instill in your family.

Reflection: The Mark You Want to Leave

Legacy starts with reflection. Take a moment to think about the mark you want to leave on the world. Ask yourself:

- What values do I want to pass on?
- What impact do I want to have on my family, my community, and the world?
- What do I want people to remember about me?

For me, it always comes back to making a positive impact. I want to be remembered as someone who helped others grow, who inspired people to see their potential, and who showed up with authenticity and kindness, and who made you laugh along the way. Legacy isn't about perfection; it's about intention.

Practical Steps to Live Intentionally

Living a legacy-worthy life isn't about waiting until the end to make your mark. It's about the choices you make every day. Here are some practical ways to live intentionally:

1. **Align Your Actions with Your Values:** Take stock of how you're spending your time and energy. Are your actions reflecting what matters most to you?

2. **Mentor and Teach:** Share your knowledge, experiences, and lessons with others. Legacy is often built in the relationships we nurture and the wisdom we pass on.

3. **Create a Ripple Effect:** Look for ways to contribute to your community, whether it's volunteering, mentoring, or simply showing up with kindness.

4. **Document Your Journey:** Write down your thoughts, values, and stories. These become a treasure trove for those who come after you.

5. **Be Present:** Legacy isn't just about what you leave behind—it's about how you show up in the here and now. Presence is a gift that leaves a lasting impression.

A Personal Story: Legacy in Action

I remember a time when I was facilitating a leadership retreat. As we wrapped up, one participant stood up and shared how the experience had completely shifted their perspective—not just on their work, but on their life. They said, "You helped me see who I want to be." That moment hit me hard because it reminded me that legacy isn't just about what you accomplish—it's about the lives you touch along the way.

And then there's Katherine Whitteman, my neighbor growing up. Katherine's legacy to me wasn't built in big, flashy moments—it was built at her kitchen table. After school, on weekends, or vacation days, I would go to her house and feel completely cared for. I can still remember how she'd draw a paper watch in pencil, carefully cut it out, and tape it to my wrist every afternoon. For some reason wearing a watch made me feel important (I guess I didn't realize it wasn't a working one at this point). She made certain foods because she knew I loved them. And she'd listen—really listen—looking me in the eye as if nothing in the world mattered more in that moment. To me, her legacy is one of kindness, love, and respect. It reminds me that legacy doesn't have to be far-reaching or grandiose. It can be as simple as making a child feel seen, safe, loved and valued.

Why Legacy Matters

Legacy isn't just about leaving something behind, it's about living fully in the present. It's about being intentional with your growth, your choices, and your impact. When you live with purpose, you inspire others to do the same. Your legacy becomes a beacon, showing what's possible when we commit to growth.

Your Turn: Rooted in Legacy

So, what's your legacy? Take a moment to reflect on the mark you want to leave. Write it down, speak it out loud, or share it with someone you trust. And then, start living it—one intentional step at a time. Because legacy isn't built in a day—it's built in the choices you make every day. And trust me, those choices have the power to change the world.

Chapter 11
Seasons of Growth

Growth is a beautiful thing—but let's be honest, it doesn't look or feel the same all the time. If you've ever tried to force yourself to be "on" every single day, you already know what I'm talking about. Growth has seasons, just like nature does. There are times for planting new ideas, moments of rapid blooming, hard-earned harvests, and yes, even stretches of dormancy when nothing seems to be happening.

For the longest time, I thought growth meant going full speed ahead all the time. I was constantly planting, constantly hustling, and constantly burning myself out. But life, much like my ill-fated attempts at gardening, had other plans. I remember one particularly tough season when everything felt stuck. It was like my roots were frozen in place, and no amount of effort seemed to make a difference. At first, I panicked. Was I failing? Had I peaked? But then I realized something: I wasn't stuck- I was resting. I was in my winter season, gathering strength for what would come next.

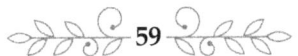

Here's the truth about seasons of growth: they all matter. The blooming and harvesting get all the glory, but the planting and resting? That's where the magic happens. Without those quieter seasons, there's no foundation for the bright, showy growth to take root.

Let's start with planting. This is the season of possibilities. It's when you're trying new things, setting goals, and dreaming big. It's exciting, sure, but it's also messy. Not every seed you plant will grow, and that's okay. Think of this as the trial-and-error phase of growth. For me, planting often looks like brainstorming ideas, diving into new projects, and saying yes to opportunities that scare me a little. It's not perfect, but it's hopeful, and that's what matters.

Then there's growth—the part everyone loves to talk about. Growth is when things finally start happening. Your efforts take root, your energy is high, and you feel unstoppable. But here's the thing about growth: it's demanding. It requires focus, discipline, and, honestly, a good dose of patience. Growth doesn't happen overnight. It's more like watching a plant grow in slow motion— thrilling, but also a little maddening if you're the impatient type (like me).

Harvesting is the reward for all that hard work. It's when you get to enjoy the fruits of your labor, whether

that's a new job, a healed relationship, or simply the satisfaction of knowing you showed up for yourself. But harvesting isn't just about reaping the rewards; it's also about reflection. What worked? What didn't? What do you want to carry forward into your next season?

And finally, we come to resting. This is the season we're least comfortable with because it feels like nothing's happening. But resting isn't stagnation—it's restoration. It's the time your roots need to recover from the effort of growing and blooming. Without rest, the soil of your life becomes depleted, and growth becomes impossible. Resting looks different for everyone. For me, it's time with family, journaling, and giving myself permission to just be. No goals, no hustle—just stillness.

Whatever season you're in right now, honor it. If you're planting, be brave enough to try. If you're growing, lean into the challenge. If you're harvesting, celebrate how far you've come. And if you're resting, embrace the pause. Every season has its purpose, and together, they create the rhythm of a life in full bloom.

Because here's the thing: growth isn't linear, and it's not constant. It's cyclical, a beautiful dance of effort and renewal. And when you learn to move with the seasons instead of fighting against them, that's when growth becomes sustainable—and joyful.

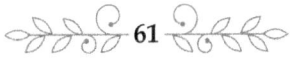

Chapter 12
A Life in Full Bloom

From the moment we planted the seed with the analogy of being rootbound, we've been on a journey together—a journey of growth, courage, and transformation. We've explored what it means to break free from constraints, expand our containers, and nurture the roots of our values and purpose. And now, here we are, standing tall ready to bloom. Or, perhaps, standing with our hands dirty and our faces a little sweaty, surrounded by awareness that our pot might need to be addressed, and unsure of what to do next. Trust yourself, your answers are coming.

Reiterating the Journey: From Rootbound to Thriving

If you've ever felt stuck, like your life had outgrown the pot you were living in, you're not alone. Growth starts with recognizing that feeling of being rootbound. It's the discomfort that whispers, "There's more for you than this." It's the moment you realize that staying in the same small container is no longer an option.

Growth is messy. It's uncomfortable, uncertain, and sometimes downright exhausting. You'll re-pot yourself, find a new container, and then realize that container needs to be expanded again. That's the nature of growth—it's a cycle, not a one-time event. And while the work is hard, it's also incredibly rewarding. Growth isn't about perfection; it's about progress.

Embracing Your Own Growth Journey

Here's my invitation to you: embrace your own growth journey. Whether you're just starting to realize you're rootbound or you're already standing tall in full bloom, your journey matters. Growth doesn't have a finish line, it's an ongoing process of learning, adapting, and becoming. And the beauty of it is that no two journeys look the same.

Take a moment to reflect: What's calling you to grow? What's been whispering, "It's time for more" in your life? Listen to those whispers. They're your invitation to step into something bigger.

The Ongoing Nature of Growth

There was a time when I thought I had "made it." I'd hit a big milestone, and for a moment, I let myself believe I could just settle in and enjoy the view. But life had other plans. New challenges arose, and I realized that staying in one place—mentally, emotionally, or spiritually—wasn't an option. Growth called me forward, as it always does. And while it wasn't easy, it was worth it. Each step forward added another layer to my story, my impact, and my legacy. The same is true for you.

As we wrap up this journey together, I want to leave you with this: growth is one of the greatest gifts you can give yourself. It's not always comfortable, but it's always worth it. Each time you choose to grow, you're not just changing your own life, you're impacting the lives of everyone around you. Your courage to expand inspires others to do the same. Your decision to bloom creates ripples that extend far beyond what you can see.

So, if you're feeling stuck, remember this: you were made for more. Your roots are deep, your potential is limitless, and the world needs what only you can bring. Keep growing, keep blooming, and never stop believing in the beauty of your own journey. Because a life in full bloom? That's a life worth living.

Now, go forth and grow, my friends. The world is waiting for your brilliance.

About the author

MaryBeth "MB" Gustitus is an Integrative Coach, speaker, and personal development facilitator with a passion for helping people break free from feeling stuck and step into their fullest potential. With a career rooted in coaching, entrepreneurship, and high-performance development, she has guided countless individuals through the discomfort of outgrowing old roles, relationships, and mindsets. Rootbound was born from her own journey of realizing she had outgrown parts of her life and needed the courage to expand into something bigger.

When she's not coaching or writing, MB finds joy and inspiration being with her family and friends, in nature or in a plant store, (convincing herself that this will be the houseplant she actually keeps alive). She invites readers to connect with her at Mile1Coaching. com or on social media, because growth is always better when we do it together.

www.ingramcontent.com/pod-product-compliance
Lightning Source LLC
Chambersburg PA
CBHW061716120626
46550CB00003B/1252